영어 리딩 학습의 최[종 목표는 독해]력 향상에 있습니다.

학년이 올라갈수록 영어 시험 출제의 비중이 높아지는 논픽션. 우리는 논픽션 리딩을 통해 다양한 분야의 어휘와 지식을 습득하고 문제 해결 능력을 키울 수 있습니다. 또한 생활 속 실용문과 시험 상황의 복잡한 지문을 이해하고 분석하며, 나에게 필요한 정보를 추출하는 연습을 할 수 있습니다. 논픽션 독해력은 비판적 사고와 논리적 사고를 발전시키고, 영어로 표현된 아이디어를 깊이 있게 이해하고 효과적으로 소통하는 언어 능력을 갖출 수 있도록 도와줍니다.

미국교과서는 논픽션 리딩에 가장 적합한 학습 도구입니다.

미국교과서는 과학, 사회과학, 역사, 예술, 문학 등 다양한 주제의 폭넓은 지식과 이해를 제공하며, 사실을 그대로 받아들이는 능력뿐만 아니라 텍스트 너머의 맥락에 대한 비판적 사고와 분석 능력도 함께 배울 수 있도록 구성되어 있습니다. 미국 교과과정 주제의 리딩을 통해 학생들은 현실적인 주제를 탐구하고, 아카데믹한 어휘를 학습하면서 논리적 탐구의 방법을 함께 배울 수 있습니다. 미국교과서는 논픽션 독해력 향상을 위한 최고의 텍스트입니다.

탁월한 논픽션 독해력을 원한다면
미국교과서 READING 시리즈

① 미국교과서의 핵심 주제들을 엄선하여 담은 지문을 읽으며 **독해력**이 향상되고 **배경지식**이 쌓입니다.

② 가지고 있는 지식과 새로운 정보를 연결해 내 것으로 만드는 **통합사고력**을 기를 수 있습니다.

③ 꼼꼼히 읽고 완전히 소화할 수 있도록 하는 수준별 독해 훈련으로 **문제 해결력**이 향상됩니다.

④ 기초 문장 독해에서 추론까지, 학습자의 **수준별로 선택하여 학습**할 수 있도록 난이도를 설계하였습니다.

⑤ 스스로 계획하고 점검하며 실력을 쌓아가는 **자기주도력**이 형성됩니다.

Author Contents Tree

Contents Tree has published various English learning textbooks and teacher's guides. It also provides an English Reading Specialist Training Course for English teachers. At the same time, Contents Tree runs an English Reading Library named Reader's Mate.

미국교과서 **READING LEVEL 1 ❶**
American Textbook Reading *Second Edition*

Second Published on August 14, 2023
Third Printed on July 15, 2024

First Published on July 18, 2016

Written by Contents Tree
Editorial Manager Namhui Kim, Seulgi Han
Development Editor Mina Park
Proofreading Ryan P. Lagace, Benjamin Schultz
Design Kichun Jang, Hyeonsook Lee
Typesetting Yeon Design
Illustrations Eunhyung Ryu, Heeju Joe
Recording Studio YR Media
Photo Credit Photos.com, Shutterstcok.com

Published and distributed by Gilbutschool

56, Worldcup-ro 10-gil, Mapo-gu, Seoul, Korea, 121-842
Tel 02-332-0931
Fax 02-322-0586
Homepage www.gilbutschool.co.kr
Publisher Jongwon Lee

ISBN   979-11-6406-538-7 (64740)
       979-11-6406-535-6 (set)
(Gilbutschool code : 30536)

미국교과서 리딩

READING

LEVEL 1 ①

길벗스쿨

LEVEL 1 논픽션 리딩 준비

리딩의 기초가 되는 언어 실력을 키울 수 있는 학습 요소를 중점적으로 익힙니다.

영어 학습의 기초 능력을 다지는 시기로서 지문에 등장할 어휘를 미리 숙지하고 패턴 문형을 반복적으로 눈과 귀로 익혀, 리딩을 수월히 소화할 수 있도록 구성하였습니다.

미국 프리스쿨 과정의 일상 주제와 기초 논픽션 주제 어휘를 학습합니다.

● 권별 주제 구성

1권	2권	3권
1. Body Parts	13. Rain	25. Tree
2. My Brother	14. Spring	26. Housework
3. Family	15. Things in Pairs	27. Riding a Bike
4. My School	16. Animal Homes	28. Spider
5. Animals	17. Community	29. Hobbies
6. Seasons	18. My Room	30. Winter
7. Things in the Sky	19. Bad Dream	31. Vegetables
8. Shapes	20. Colors	32. Sea
9. Clothes	21. Food	33. My Town
10. Monsters	22. Transportation	34. School Tools
11. Jobs	23. Friends	35. Farm Animals
12. Museum	24. Sense of Touch	36. Five Senses

필수 패턴 문형이 반복되는 지문을 읽으며 문장 구조에 익숙해집니다.

글의 주제와 가벼운 의미 파악 수준의 기초 독해 연습으로 리딩의 기본기를 만듭니다.

· 자기주도 학습 계획표 ·

	Study Check		Day
Unit 1	Get Ready	☐	/
	Now You Read	☐	/
	Check Up	☐	/
	Workbook	☐	/
Unit 2	Get Ready	☐	/
	Now You Read	☐	/
	Check Up	☐	/
	Workbook	☐	/
Unit 3	Get Ready	☐	/
	Now You Read	☐	/
	Check Up	☐	/
	Workbook	☐	/
Unit 4	Get Ready	☐	/
	Now You Read	☐	/
	Check Up	☐	/
	Workbook	☐	/
Unit 5	Get Ready	☐	/
	Now You Read	☐	/
	Check Up	☐	/
	Workbook	☐	/
Unit 6	Get Ready	☐	/
	Now You Read	☐	/
	Check Up	☐	/
	Workbook	☐	/

	Study Check		Day
Unit 7	Get Ready	☐	/
	Now You Read	☐	/
	Check Up	☐	/
	Workbook	☐	/
Unit 8	Get Ready	☐	/
	Now You Read	☐	/
	Check Up	☐	/
	Workbook	☐	/
Unit 9	Get Ready	☐	/
	Now You Read	☐	/
	Check Up	☐	/
	Workbook	☐	/
Unit 10	Get Ready	☐	/
	Now You Read	☐	/
	Check Up	☐	/
	Workbook	☐	/
Unit 11	Get Ready	☐	/
	Now You Read	☐	/
	Check Up	☐	/
	Workbook	☐	/
Unit 12	Get Ready	☐	/
	Now You Read	☐	/
	Check Up	☐	/
	Workbook	☐	/

Get Ready

기초 단어와 핵심 패턴 문형을 익히며 글의 소재를 알아보고,
문장 구조에 익숙해집니다.

QR코드를 스캔하여 정확한 발음 확인하기

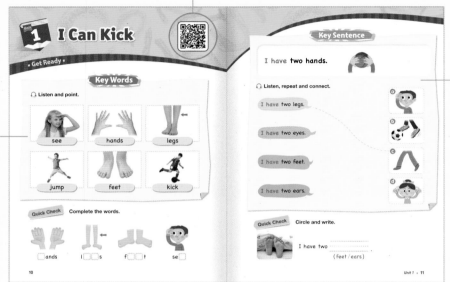

Key Words

주제별 단어를
듣고, 따라 말하며
익힙니다.

Key Sentence

글에서 접하게 될
패턴 문형을 미리
학습합니다.

Now You Read

일상생활, 학교생활 주제의 글을 읽으며 기초 독해력을 쌓고,
어휘와 문장에 익숙해집니다.

Reading Passage

그림을 통해 내용을
먼저 예측해 본 후,
음원을 듣고, 따라
읽으며 세부 내용을
파악합니다.

Pop Quiz

그림, 사진 관련
퀴즈를 풀며 글의
내용을 다시 한 번
떠올려 봅니다.

Check Up

다양한 유형의 문제를 풀며 읽은 내용을 확인하고,
단어와 문장을 점검합니다.

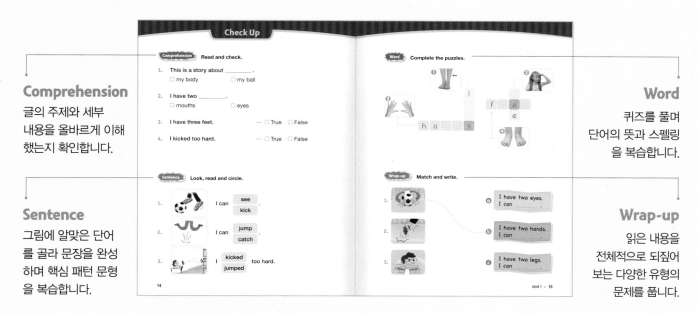

Comprehension
글의 주제와 세부
내용을 올바르게 이해
했는지 확인합니다.

Sentence
그림에 알맞은 단어
를 골라 문장을 완성
하며 핵심 패턴 문형
을 복습합니다.

Word
퀴즈를 풀며
단어의 뜻과 스펠링
을 복습합니다.

Wrap-up
읽은 내용을
전체적으로 되짚어
보는 다양한 유형의
문제를 풉니다.

Workbook

단어와 패턴 문형을
복습합니다.

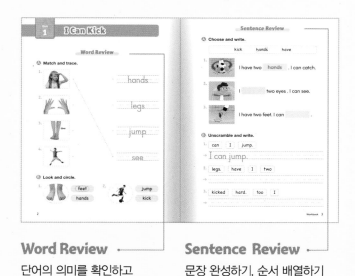

Word Review
단어의 의미를 확인하고
쓰면서 복습합니다.

Sentence Review
문장 완성하기, 순서 배열하기
활동으로 패턴 문형과 어순을
복습합니다.

무료 온라인 학습 자료

길벗스쿨 e클래스
(eclass.gilbut.co.kr)에
접속하시면 〈미국교과서
READING〉 시리즈에 대한
상세 정보 및 부가 학습 자료를
무료로 이용하실 수 있습니다.

1. 음원 스트리밍 및 MP3 파일
2. 추가 학습용 워크시트 5종
   단어 카드, 단어 테스트, 문장 따라 쓰기,
   리딩 지문 테스트, 문장 테스트
3. 복습용 온라인 퀴즈

★ 목차 ★

Unit 1 **I Can Kick** Body Parts

Key Sentence I have two hands.

10

Unit 2 **My Little Brother** My Brother

Key Sentence I help him drink.

16

Unit 3 **This Is My Family** Family

Key Sentence This is my family.

22

Unit 4 **School Is Fun** My School

Key Sentence I read books.

28

Unit 5 **Animals at Night** Animals

Key Sentence Some animals move at night.

34

Unit 6 **The Four Seasons** Seasons

Key Sentence I go fishing.

40

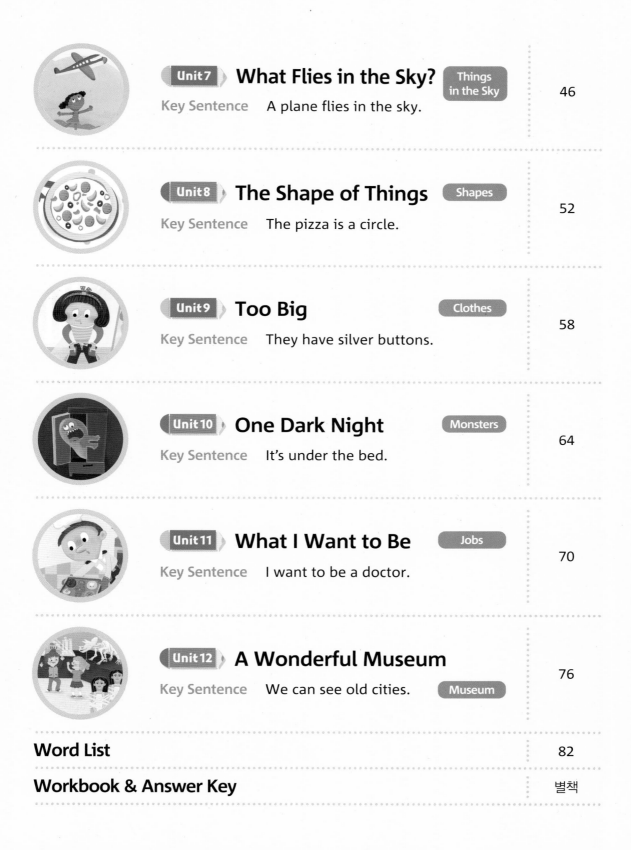

Unit 7 **What Flies in the Sky?** Things in the Sky

Key Sentence   A plane flies in the sky.

46

Unit 8 **The Shape of Things** Shapes

Key Sentence   The pizza is a circle.

52

Unit 9 **Too Big** Clothes

Key Sentence   They have silver buttons.

58

Unit 10 **One Dark Night** Monsters

Key Sentence   It's under the bed.

64

Unit 11 **What I Want to Be** Jobs

Key Sentence   I want to be a doctor.

70

Unit 12 **A Wonderful Museum**

Key Sentence   We can see old cities. Museum

76

Word List   82

Workbook & Answer Key   별책

I Can Kick

• Get Ready •

Key Words

🎧 **Listen and point.**

see

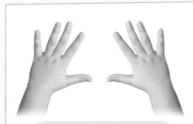

hands

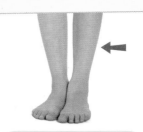

legs

jump

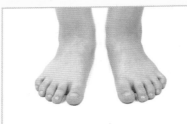

feet

kick

Quick Check   **Complete the words.**

☐ ands

l ☐ ☐ s

f ☐ ☐ t

se ☐

I have **two hands.**

🎧 **Listen, repeat and connect.**

I have two legs.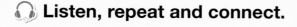

I have two eyes.

I have two feet.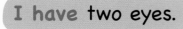

I have two ears.

Quick Check   **Circle and write.**

I have two _____ .

(feet / ears)

I Can Kick

I **have** two eyes.

I can see.

    I **have** two hands.

    I can catch.

12

I have two legs.
I can jump.

I have two feet.
I can kick.

Oh, no!
I kicked too hard.

Pop Quiz

What is the boy
playing now?

Comprehension   **Read and check.**

1. This is a story about _____ .
   ☐ my body   ☐ my ball

2. I have two _____ .
   ☐ mouths   ☐ eyes

3. I have three feet.   ⋯ ☐ True   ☐ False

4. I kicked too hard.   ⋯ ☐ True   ☐ False

Sentence   **Look, read and circle.**

1.  I can
   see
   kick
   .

2.  I can
   jump
   catch
   .

3.  I
   kicked
   jumped
   too hard.

Word Complete the puzzles.

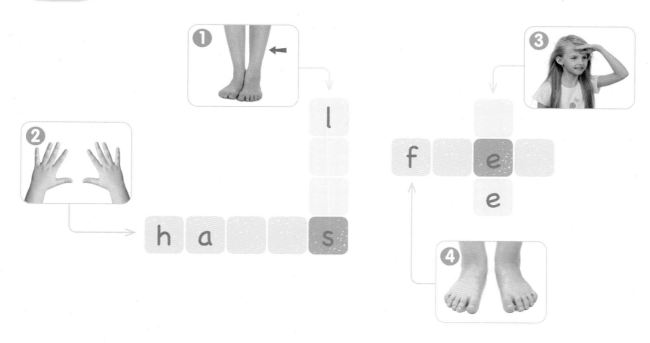

Wrap-up Match and write.

1.

2.

3.

ⓐ I have two eyes.
I can _____.

ⓑ I have two hands.
I can _____.

ⓒ I have two legs.
I can _____.

Unit 2 My Little Brother

• Get Ready •

Key Words

🎧 **Listen and point.**

baby

brother

eat

walk

sit

sleep

Quick Check   **Complete the words.**

b ☐ by

☐☐ eep

w ☐ lk

ea ☐

Key Sentence

I help him **drink.**

🎧 **Listen, repeat and connect.**

I help him eat.

I help him walk.

I help him sit down.

I help him sleep.

a

b

c

d

Quick Check Circle and write.

I help him _____ .

(walk / eat)

My Little Brother 🎧

This is my baby brother.
I help him every day.

I help him drink.
I help him eat.

18

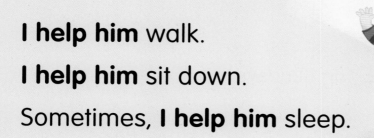

I help him walk.

I help him sit down.

Sometimes, **I help him** sleep.

I love my little brother.

Comprehension Read and check.

1. This is a story about _____ .
   ☐ my baby sister   ☐ my baby brother

2. I help him _____ .
   ☐ every day   ☐ on Sundays

3. Sometimes, I help him sleep.   ··· ☐ True   ☐ False

4. I help him cry.   ··· ☐ True   ☐ False

Sentence Look, read and circle.

1.  I help him
   walk
   sit down
   .

2.  I help him
   drink
   eat
   .

3.  I
   love
   draw
   my little brother.

20

Find and circle.

① walk

w	n	h	p	b	a	b	y
a	e	s	o	a	q	e	i
l	e	s	l	e	e	p	k
k	a	e	e	n	f	a	h
a	t	o	n	g	c	m	g

③ baby

② sleep

④ eat

Wrap-up **Look and write.**

1. I help him _____ .

2. I help him _____ .

4. I help him _____ .

3. I help him _____ .

Unit 3 This Is My Family

Key Words

🎧 Listen and point.

family

father

mother

sister

student

dog

Quick Check

Complete the words.

☐ amily

sis ☐ er

fath ☐☐

☐☐ udent

This is my **family.**

🎧 **Listen, repeat and connect.**

This is my father.

This is my mother.

This is my sister.

This is my dog.

 a

 b

 c

 d

Quick Check **Circle and write.**

 This is my _____ .

(father / sister)

This Is My Family

Look at this picture.

This is my family.

This is my father.

He is a cook.

24

This is my mother.

She is a teacher.

This is my sister, Jane.

Jane and I are students at this school.

And **this is my** dog, Doogie.

Pop Quiz

What does Jane have in the picture?

Comprehension   **Read and check.**

1. This is a story about _____ .
    ☐ my school   ☐ my family

2. This is my _____ , Doogie.
    ☐ cat   ☐ dog

3. My father is a teacher.   ⋯ ☐ True   ☐ False

4. My sister is a student.   ⋯ ☐ True   ☐ False

Sentence   **Look, read and circle.**

1.    This is my   mother
                                         brother   .

2.    This is my   sister
                                         father   .

3.    Jane and I are   students
                                            teachers   .

Word **Complete the puzzle.**

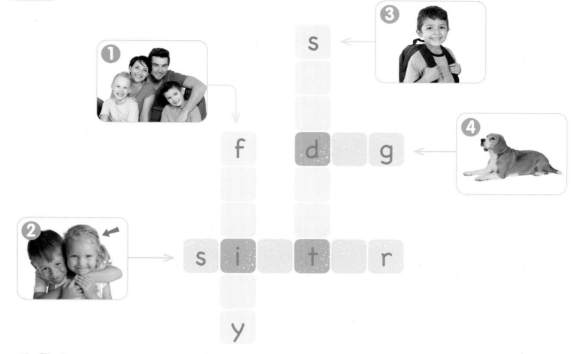

Wrap-up **Look and write.**

1. My father is a _____ .

2. My mother is a _____ .

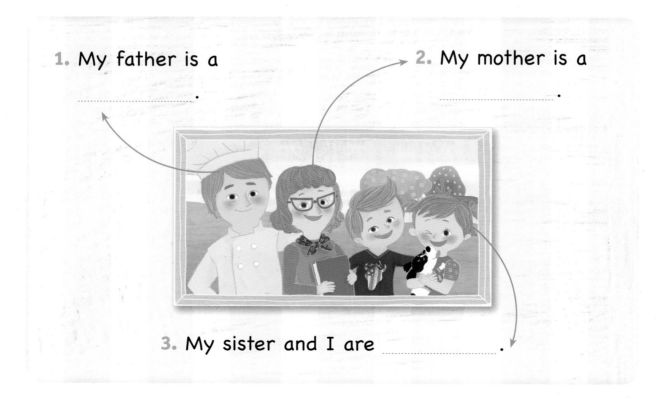

3. My sister and I are _____ .

School Is Fun

Key Words

🎧 **Listen and point.**

school

read

write

draw

sing

play

Quick Check   **Complete the words.**

☐☐ aw

wr ☐ te

☐ ead

sin ☐

I read **books.**

🎧 **Listen, repeat and connect.**

I write stories.

I draw pictures.

I sing songs.

I eat my lunch.

Quick Check  Circle and write.

I _____ pictures.

(play / draw)

School Is Fun

This is my school.

I have so much fun at school.

I read books.

I write stories.

I draw pictures.

I sing songs.

I play with my friends.

I eat my lunch.

It's time to go home.

See you tomorrow!

What is the girl eating?

Comprehension   **Read and check.**

1. This is a story about _____ .

   ☐ my house   ☐ my school

2. I _____ pictures.

   ☐ read   ☐ draw

3. I have so much fun at school.   ⋯ ☐ True   ☐ False

4. I play with my brothers at school.   ⋯ ☐ True   ☐ False

Sentence   **Look, read and circle.**

1.  I   write / play   stories.

2.  I   sing / draw   songs.

3.  This is my   school / lunch .

Word **Find and circle.**

draw

q	w	e	r	r	i	f	a
a	s	s	c	d	r	a	w
w	r	i	t	e	e	z	t
e	g	n	u	i	a	b	e
g	j	g	h	j	d	m	p

write

read

sing

 **Wrap-up** **Look and write.**

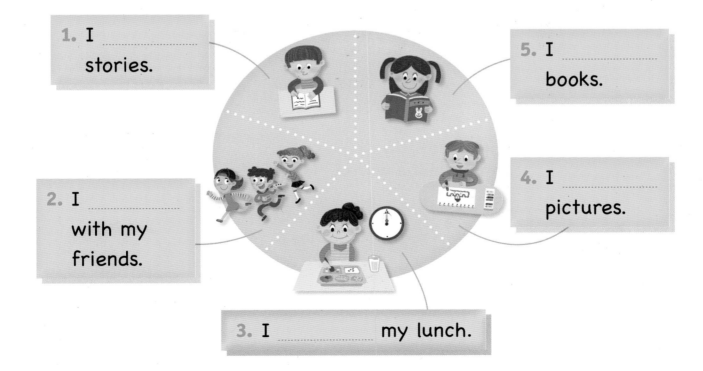

1. I _____ stories.

5. I _____ books.

2. I _____ with my friends.

4. I _____ pictures.

3. I _____ my lunch.

Animals at Night

• Get Ready •

Key Words

🎧 **Listen and point.**

night

owl

catch

bat

tiger

hunt

Quick Check **Complete the words.**

☐wl

cat☐☐

ti☐er

nig☐☐

34

Key Sentence

Some animals move at night.

🎧 **Listen, repeat and connect.**

Owls move at night.

Bats move at night.

Tigers move at night.

Cats move at night.

Quick Check **Circle and write.**

_____ move at night.

(Owls / Bats)

Animals at Night

Some animals **move at night**.

Owls **move at night**.
They catch mice in the dark.

Pop Quiz

What is the owl catching?

Bats **move at night**.

They eat fruits in the dark.

Tigers **move at night**.

They hunt deer in the dark.

Do you **move at night**, too?

Comprehension   Read and check.

1. **This is a story about _____ .**
    ☐ animals at night   ☐ animals at the zoo

2. **_____ move at night.**
    ☐ Butterflies   ☐ Tigers

3. **Bats move at night.**   ··· ☐ True   ☐ False

4. **Owls hunt deer in the dark.**   ··· ☐ True   ☐ False

Sentence   Look, read and circle.

1.    **Some animals move at** | noon |
                                                    | night | **.**

2.    **They eat** | fruits |
                                        | owls | **in the dark.**

3.    **They catch** | mice |
                                          | deer | **in the dark.**

Complete the puzzles.

1

n

t i   r

2

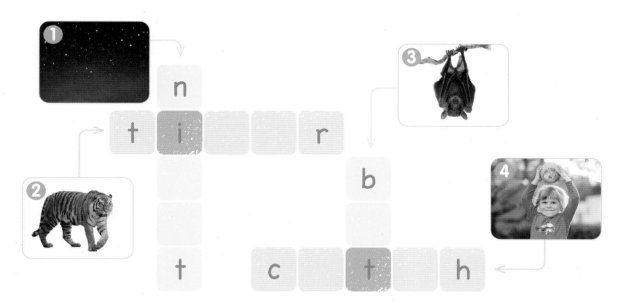

3

b

t

t   c   t   h

4

Match and write.

1.

2.

3.

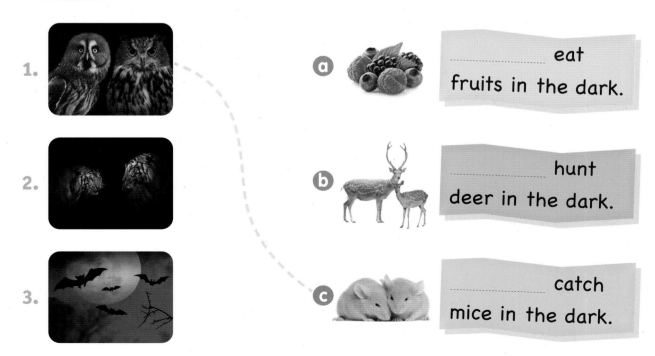

a   _____ eat fruits in the dark.

b   _____ hunt deer in the dark.

c   _____ catch mice in the dark.

The Four Seasons

- **Get Ready** -

Key Words

🎧 **Listen and point.**

spring

warm

summer

hot

fall

winter

Quick Check **Complete the words.**

☐ pring

su ☐ mer

fa ☐ l

win ☐ er

I go fishing.

🎧 **Listen, repeat and connect.**

I go swimming.

I go camping.

I go skating.

I go skiing.

Quick Check   **Circle and write.**

I go _____ .

(skating / swimming)

The Four Seasons 🎧

It is spring.

The weather is warm.

I go fish**ing**.

It is summer.

The weather is hot.

I go swimm**ing**.

42

It is fall.

The weather is cool.

I go camp**ing**.

It is winter.

The weather is cold.

I go skat**ing**.

Pop Quiz

How many kids are fishing?

Comprehension Read and check.

1. This is a story about _____.

    ☐ four friends   ☐ four seasons

2. It is spring. I go _____.

    ☐ fishing   ☐ skating

3. It is summer. The weather is cold.   ··· ☐ True   ☐ False

4. It is fall. The weather is cool.   ··· ☐ True   ☐ False

Sentence Look, read and circle.

1.    I go   swimming / skating .

2.    I go   camping / fishing .

3.    The weather is   hot / cold .

Find and circle.

spring

winter

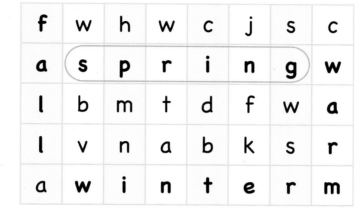

f	w	h	w	c	j	s	c
a	s	p	r	i	n	g	w
l	b	m	t	d	f	w	a
l	v	n	a	b	k	s	r
a	w	i	n	t	e	r	m

warm

fall

Wrap-up **Look and write.**

1. I go _____ .

2. I go _____ .

3. I go _____ .

4. I go _____ .

What Flies in the Sky?

Get Ready

Key Words

🎧 Listen and point.

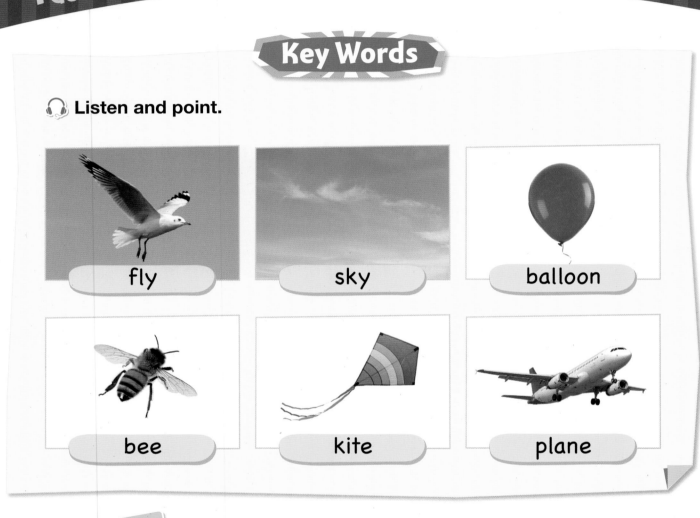

fly

sky

balloon

bee

kite

plane

Quick Check Complete the words.

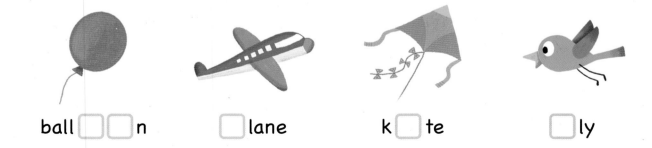

ball ☐☐ n   ☐ lane   k ☐ te   ☐ ly

Key Sentence

A plane flies in the sky.

🎧 **Listen, repeat and connect.**

A balloon flies in the sky.

A bee flies in the sky.

A kite flies in the sky.

A bird flies in the sky.

 **a**

 **b**

 **c**

 **d**

Quick Check Circle and write.

A _____ flies in the sky.

(bee / kite)

What Flies in the Sky?

Can you see that?

What **flies in the sky**?

A balloon **flies in the sky**.

A bee **flies in the sky**.

A kite **flies in the sky**.

A plane **flies in the sky**.

I wish I could fly in the sky!

Pop Quiz

What color is the balloon?

Comprehension Read and check.

1. This is a story about what flies in the _____ .
   ☐ water   ☐ sky

2. A _____ flies in the sky.
   ☐ balloon   ☐ tiger

3. A bee flies in the sky.   ⋯ ☐ True   ☐ False

4. I wish I could swim in the sky!   ⋯ ☐ True   ☐ False

Sentence Look, read and circle.

1.
   A kite / balloon flies in the sky.

2.
   A bird / plane flies in the sky.

3.
   I wish I could fly / run in the sky!

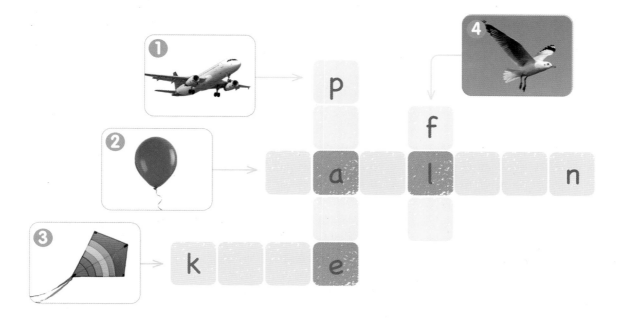

Wrap-up Read and circle the correct ones.

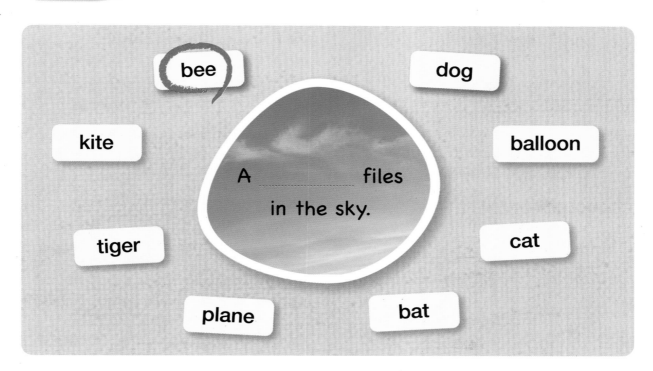

bee

dog

kite

balloon

A _____ files in the sky.

tiger

cat

plane

bat

The Shape of Things

▪ Get Ready ▪

Key Words

🎧 **Listen and point.**

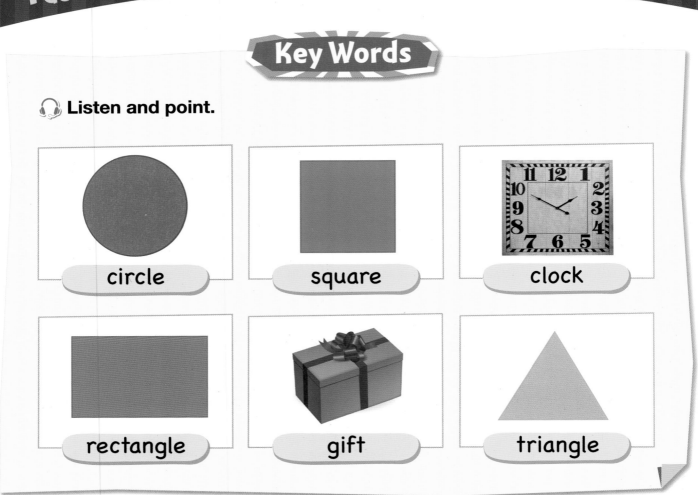

circle	square	clock
rectangle	gift	triangle

Quick Check **Complete the words.**

 ☐☐iangle

 ☐☐ock

 ☐ift

 ☐ircle

52

The pizza is **a circle.**

🎧 **Listen, repeat and connect.**

The clock is a square.

The plate is a circle.

The party hat is a triangle.

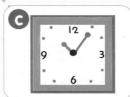

The gift box is a rectangle.

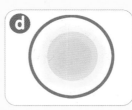

 **Circle and write.**

The gift box is a _____ .

(triangle / rectangle)

The Shape of Things

Shapes are everywhere.
Let's find them.

What is a circle?
The pizza is a circle.

What is a square?
The clock is a square.

What is a rectangle?
The gift box is a rectangle.

What is a triangle?
The party hat is a triangle.

Pop Quiz

What time is it now?

Read and check.

1. This is a story about the _____ of things.
   ☐ shape   ☐ color

2. The pizza is a _____.
   ☐ square   ☐ circle

3. Shapes are everywhere.   ⋯ ☐ True   ☐ False

4. The gift box is a triangle.   ⋯ ☐ True   ☐ False

Sentence **Look, read and circle.**

1.
   Shapes
   Clocks
   are everywhere.

2.
   The party hat is a   circle
                        triangle .

3.
   The clock is a   rectangle
                    square .

①

gift

②

circle

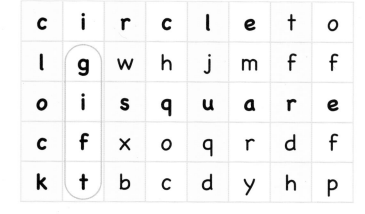

c	i	r	c	l	e	t	o
l	g	w	h	j	m	f	f
o	i	s	q	u	a	r	e
c	f	x	o	q	r	d	f
k	t	b	c	d	y	h	p

③

square

④

clock

Wrap-up   **Match and write.**

1.

2.

3.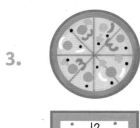

4.

ⓐ The pizza is a _____ .

ⓑ The clock is a _____ .

ⓒ The gift box is a _____ .

ⓓ The party hat is a _____ .

Key Words

🎧 **Listen and point.**

pants

silver

button

ribbon

pocket

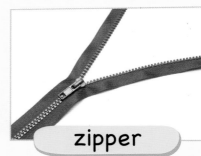

zipper

Quick Check **Complete the words.**

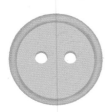

☐utton

pocke☐

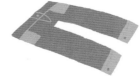

☐ants

☐ipper

Key Sentence

They have **silver buttons.**

🎧 **Listen, repeat and connect.**

They have **big pockets.**

They have **nice zippers.**

It has **a yellow ribbon.**

It has **red lace.**

Quick Check Circle and write.

It has big _____ .

(pockets / ribbons)

Too Big

I like these pants.

They will look good on me.

They have silver buttons.

They have a yellow ribbon.

They have big pockets.

They have nice zippers.

They will be perfect for me.

Oh, no!

They are too big!

Unit 9 • 61

Pop Quiz

How many silver buttons are on the pants?

Check Up

Comprehension   **Read and check.**

1. This is a story about _____ .
    ☐ my pants   ☐ my shirt

2. I _____ these pants.
    ☐ like   ☐ draw

3. They have silver buttons.   ⋯ ☐ True   ☐ False

4. They are too small!   ⋯ ☐ True   ☐ False

Sentence   **Look, read and circle.**

1.  It has a yellow [button / ribbon] .

2.  They have big [ribbons / pockets] .

3.  They have nice [zippers / buttons] .

Complete the puzzle.

s i   r

b   t   n

p o   e

Look and write.

I like these pants.

1. They have big
_____ .

2. They have silver
_____ .

3. They have
a yellow
_____ .

4. They have nice
_____ .

■ Get Ready ■

Key Words

🎧 **Listen and point.**

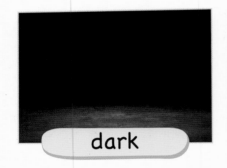
dark

monster

in

under

on

behind

Quick Check **Complete the words.**

☐onster

☐ark

un☐er

behin☐

It's under **the bed.**

🎧 **Listen, repeat and connect.**

It's on the chair.

It's in the closet.

It's behind the door.

It's on the desk.

Quick Check **Circle and write.**

It's _____ the closet.

(in / under)

One Dark Night

It is a dark night.

There are scary monsters in my room.

Sometimes, **it's under** the bed.

Sometimes, **it's on** the chair.

66

Pop Quiz

How many monsters can you see?

Sometimes, **it's in** the closet.

Sometimes, **it's behind** the door.

Honey, don't be scared.

There are no monsters

in your room.

Comprehension **Read and check.**

1. This is a story about _____ .

☐ a dark night   ☐ a rainy day

2. There are scary _____ in my room.

☐ bats   ☐ monsters

3. A monster is on the bed.   ⋯ ☐ True   ☐ False

4. A monster is in the closet.   ⋯ ☐ True   ☐ False

Sentence **Look, read and circle.**

1.  It's [on / under] the chair.

2.  It's [behind / in] the door.

3.  It is a [dark / warm] night.

behind

dark

u	p	b	e	h	i	n	d
n	s	p	e	x	a	d	a
d	h	o	u	c	g	l	r
e	f	r	d	v	s	j	k
r	m	o	n	s	t	e	r

monster

under

Wrap-up Look and write.

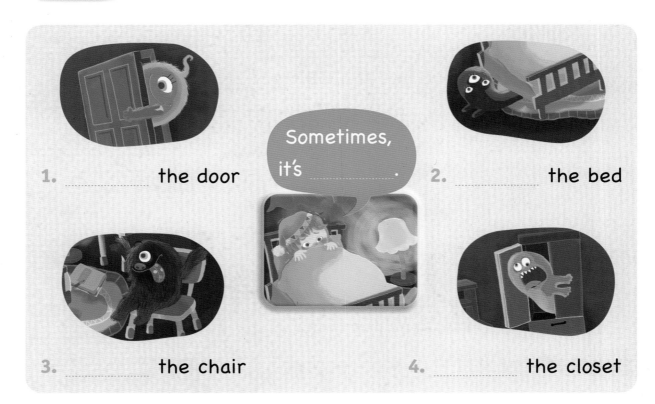

Sometimes, it's _____.

1. _____ the door

2. _____ the bed

3. _____ the chair

4. _____ the closet

What I Want to Be

■ **Get Ready** ■

Key Words

🎧 **Listen and point.**

want

doctor

baseball player

police officer

baker

many

Quick Check **Complete the words.**

☐☐ctor

b☐ker

☐ant

☐olice off☐cer

Key Sentence

I want to be **a doctor.**

🎧 **Listen, repeat and connect.**

I want to be **a baseball player.**

I want to be **a police officer.**

I want to be **a baker.**

I want to be **a singer.**

Quick Check **Circle and write.**

I want to be a _____ .

(doctor / baker)

What I Want to Be

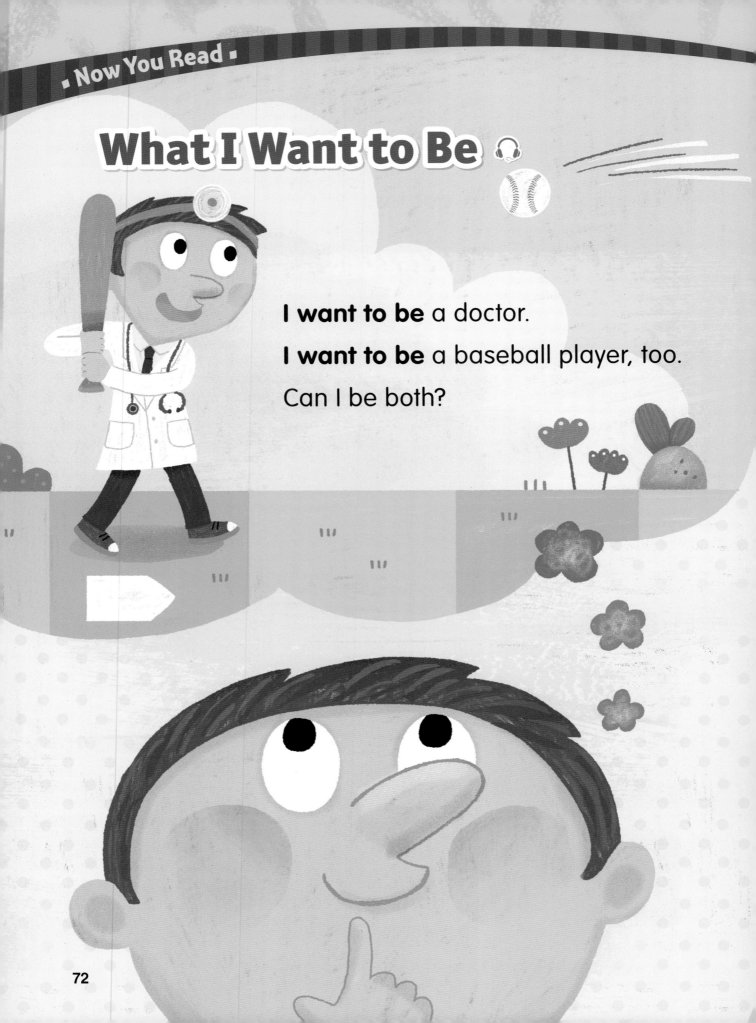

I want to be a doctor.

I want to be a baseball player, too.

Can I be both?

I want to be a police officer.

I want to be a baker, too.

Can I be both?

Oh, **I want to be** many things!

Pop Quiz

What is on the gas oven?

 **Comprehension**   Read and check.

1. This is a story about what I _____ to be.

   ☐ want   ☐ don't want

2. I want to be a _____.

   ☐ police officer   ☐ nurse

3. I want to be a teacher.   ⋯ ☐ True   ☐ False

4. I want to be many things.   ⋯ ☐ True   ☐ False

 **Sentence**   Look, read and circle.

1.    I want to be a | baseball player |
                                            | soccer player | .

2.    I want to be a | firefighter |
                                            | police officer | .

3.   I want to be | nothing |
                    | many things | .

Complete the puzzles.

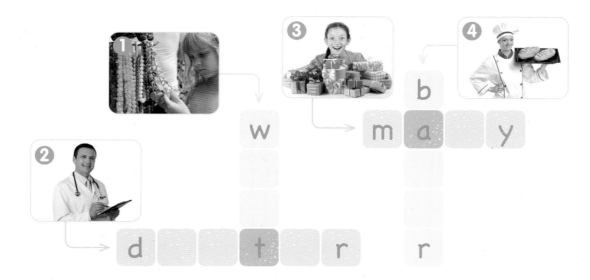

w

d o **t** r r

b

m **a** y

Read and circle the correct ones.

police officer

baker

I want to be a _____.

soccer player

singer

teacher

baseball player

doctor

A Wonderful Museum

▪ Get Ready ▪

Key Words

🎧 **Listen and point.**

museum

castle

king

queen

dinosaur

wonderful

Quick Check **Complete the words.**

☐ astle

ki ☐☐

☐ inosaur

qu ☐☐ n

Key Sentence

We can see **old cities**.

🎧 **Listen, repeat and connect.**

We can see **old castles**.

We can see **kings**.

We can see **dinosaurs**.

We can see **mummies**.

a

b

c

d

Quick Check   Circle and write.

We can see _____ .

(kings / old castles)

A Wonderful Museum

Today, we go to a museum.

What can we see?

We can see old cities.

We can see old castles.

We can see kings.

We can see queens.

We can see dinosaurs.

And **we can see** mummies.

The museum is a wonderful place.

Pop Quiz

What is the king wearing on his head?

Comprehension   **Read and check.**

1.   This is a story about _____.

   ☐ a dinosaur   ☐ a museum

2.   We can see old _____.

   ☐ cities   ☐ cars

3.   Today, we go to a museum.   ⋯ ☐ True   ☐ False

4.   We can see tigers at the museum.   ⋯ ☐ True   ☐ False

Sentence   **Look, read and circle.**

1.      We can see | dinosaurs | . | kings |

2.   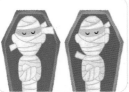   We can see | mummies | . | queens |

3.      The museum is a | wonderful | place. | scary |

80

Find and circle.

king

queen

q	c	a	s	t	l	e	k
u	n	d	e	m	n	o	i
e	x	f	j	a	o	a	n
e	r	b	d	b	t	f	g
n	y	m	u	s	e	u	m

castle

museum

Wrap-up **Look and match.**

2. We can see dinosaurs.

4. We can see old castles.

1. We can see kings.

3. We can see mummies.

a

b

c

d

WORD LIST

· Unit 1 ·		· Unit 2 ·		· Unit 3 ·	
I Can Kick		**My Little Brother**		**This Is My Family**	
☐ can	~할 수 있다	☐ baby	어린; 아기	☐ cook	요리사; 요리하다
☐ catch	잡다	☐ brother		☐ dog	개
☐ ears	귀		남자 형제(오빠, 형, 남동생)	☐ family	가족
☐ eyes	눈	☐ drink	마시다	☐ father	아빠
☐ feet	발	☐ eat	먹다	☐ look at	~을 보다
☐ hands	손	☐ every day	매일	☐ mother	엄마
☐ hard	세게, 열심히	☐ help	돕다	☐ picture	사진, 그림
☐ have	가지고 있다	☐ little	어린, 작은	☐ sister	
☐ jump	점프하다, 뛰다	☐ love	사랑하다; 사랑		여자 형제(언니, 누나, 여동생)
☐ kick	차다	☐ my	나의	☐ student	학생
☐ legs	다리	☐ sit	앉다	☐ teacher	선생님
☐ see	보다	☐ sleep	자다		
☐ too	너무	☐ sometimes	가끔, 때때로		
		☐ walk	걷다		

· Unit 4 ·
School Is Fun

- book 책
- draw 그리다
- friend 친구
- fun 재미있는; 재미
- go 가다
- home 집에; 집
- lunch 점심 식사
- play 놀다; 놀이
- read 읽다
- school 학교
- sing 노래하다
- song 노래
- story 이야기
- time 시간
- tomorrow 내일
- write 쓰다

· Unit 5 ·
Animals at Night

- animal 동물
- bat 박쥐
- dark 어둠; 어두운, 깜깜한
- deer 사슴
- fruit 과일

- hunt 사냥하다; 사냥
- mice 쥐 (mouse의 복수형)
- move 움직이다
- night 밤
- owl 올빼미, 부엉이
- some 어떤, 몇몇의
- tiger 호랑이

· Unit 6 ·
The Four Seasons

- camp 캠핑을 하다; 캠프
- cold 추운
- cool 시원한, 멋진
- fall 가을
- fish 낚시하다; 물고기
- hot 더운, 뜨거운
- season 계절
- skate 스케이트를 타다
- ski 스키를 타다
- spring 봄
- summer 여름
- swim 수영하다
- warm 따뜻한
- weather 날씨
- winter 겨울

· Unit 7 ·
What Flies in the Sky?

- balloon 풍선
- bee 벌
- bird 새
- fly 날다
- kite 연
- plane 비행기
- sky 하늘
- what 무엇
- wish 바라다; 소망

· Unit 8 ·
The Shape of Things

- box 상자
- circle 동그라미, 원형
- clock 시계
- everywhere 모든 곳에, 어디에나
- find 찾다
- gift 선물
- party hat 파티 모자
- pizza 피자
- plate 접시
- rectangle 직사각형
- shape 모양, 형태

□ square	정사각형	
□ thing	물건, 사물	
□ triangle	세모, 삼각형	

· Unit 9 ·
Too Big

□ big	큰
□ button	단추
□ good	좋은, 알맞은
□ look	~처럼 보이다, 보다
□ nice	멋진, 좋은
□ pants	바지
□ perfect	완벽한
□ pocket	주머니
□ red	빨간색(의)
□ ribbon	리본
□ silver	은색(의), 은
□ zipper	지퍼

· Unit 10 ·
One Dark Night

□ bed	침대
□ behind	~뒤에
□ chair	의자
□ closet	옷장

□ desk	책상
□ door	문
□ honey	(사랑하는 사람을 부르는 호칭) 얘, 자기
□ in	~안에
□ monster	괴물
□ on	~위에
□ room	방
□ scared	무서워하는, 겁먹은
□ scary	무서운, 겁나는
□ under	~아래에

· Unit 11 ·
What I Want to Be

□ baker	제빵사
□ baseball player	야구 선수
□ both	둘 다
□ doctor	의사
□ many	많은
□ police officer	경찰관
□ singer	가수
□ want	원하다, 바라다

· Unit 12 ·
A Wonderful Museum

□ castle	성
□ cities	도시 (city의 복수형)
□ dinosaur	공룡
□ king	왕
□ mummies	미라 (mummy의 복수형)
□ museum	박물관
□ old	낡은, 나이 많은
□ place	장소
□ queen	여왕
□ today	오늘
□ wonderful	아주 멋진, 훌륭한

미국교과서 리딩 READING

1.1

Workbook & Answer Key

길벗스쿨

미국교과서 리딩
READING

LEVEL 1 ①

Workbook

길벗스쿨

Word Review

A Match and trace.

1.

2.

3.

4.

hands

legs

jump

see

B Look and circle.

1. 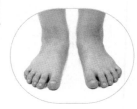   feet

hands

2.    jump

kick

Sentence Review

A **Choose and write.**

jump	hands	have

1. I have two [hands] . I can catch.

2. I [   ] two eyes . I can see.

3. I have two feet. I can [   ] .

B **Unscramble and write.**

1. | can | I | jump. |

→ I can jump.

2. | legs. | have | I | two |

→

3. | kicked | hard. | too | I |

→

My Little Brother

Word Review

A Match and trace.

1.

2.

3.

4.

eat

sleep

sit

baby

B Look and circle.

1.

walk

eat

2.

brother

baby

Sentence Review

A **Choose and write.**

help	eat	sleep

1.  I _____ him walk.

2.  Sometimes, I help him _____ .

3.  I help him _____ .

B **Unscramble and write.**

1. | help | I | sit down. | him |

→ _____

2. | brother. | This | is | baby | my |

→ _____

3. | my | love | I | brother. | little |

→ _____

This Is My Family

Word Review

A Match and trace.

1.

student

2.

father

3.

dog

4.

sister

B Look and circle.

1.

father

family

2.

mother

student

Sentence Review

A Choose and write.

dog	students	This

1. _____ is my mother.

2. Jane and I are _____ .

3. This is my _____ , Doogie.

B Unscramble and write.

1. | my | This | is | family. |

→ -

2. | a cook. | He | is |

→ -

3. | sister, | This | my | is | Jane. |

→ -

School Is Fun

Word Review

A Match and trace.

1.  •   •   sing

2.  •   •   play

3.  •   •   write

4.  •   •   school

B Look and circle.

1.    write   draw

2.    read   sing

Sentence Review

A **Choose and write.**

sing	school	draw

1. I have so much fun at _____ .

2. I _____ pictures.

3. I _____ songs.

B **Unscramble and write.**

1. | I | books. | read |

→ _____

2. | stories. | write | I |

→ _____

3. | play | with | friends. | I | my |

→ _____

Animals at Night

Word Review

 Match and trace.

1.

2.

3.

4.

bat

tiger

owl

hunt

 Look and circle.

1.

night

hunt

2.

hunt

catch

10

Sentence Review

A **Choose and write.**

Owls	move	hunt

1. Bats _____ at night.

2. They _____ deer in the dark.

3. _____ move at night.

B **Unscramble and write.**

1. | at night. | | animals | | move | | Some |

   ⇒ _____

2. | They | | mice | | catch | | in the dark. |

   ⇒ _____

3. | Do | | move | | you | | at night, | | too? |

   ⇒ _____

The Four Seasons

Word Review

A Match and trace.

1.

2.

3.

4.

fall

spring

hot

warm

B Look and circle.

1.  summer

spring

2.  fall

winter

Sentence Review

A **Choose and write.**

go	fishing	hot

1. I _____ skating.

2. The weather is _____ .

3. I go _____ .

B **Unscramble and write.**

1. [swimming.] [I] [go]

   → -

2. [go] [camping.] [I]

   → -

3. [spring.] [is] [It]

   → -

What Flies in the Sky?

Word Review

A Match and trace.

1.

2.

3.

4.

kite

plane

sky

bee

B Look and circle.

1.    fly   bee

2.    sky   balloon

Sentence Review

A Choose and write.

fly	sky	bee

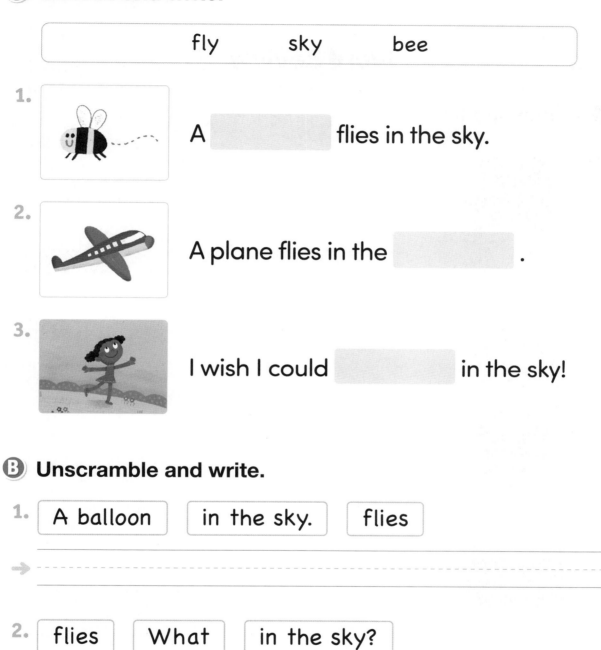

1. A _____ flies in the sky.

2. A plane flies in the _____ .

3. I wish I could _____ in the sky!

B Unscramble and write.

1. | A balloon | | in the sky. | | flies |

➔ --

2. | flies | | What | | in the sky? |

➔ --

3. | A kite | | in the sky. | | flies |

➔ --

The Shape of Things

Word Review

A Match and trace.

1.    •   • circle

2.    •   • square

3.    •   • triangle

4.    •   • rectangle

B Look and circle.

1.    circle   gift

2.   clock   triangle

Sentence Review

A **Choose and write.**

clock	triangle	rectangle

1.  The party hat is a _____ .

2.  The gift box is a _____ .

3.  The _____ is a square.

B **Unscramble and write.**

1. | are | everywhere. | Shapes |

→ _____

2. | a square? | is | What |

→ _____

3. | The pizza | a circle. | is |

→ _____

Too Big

Word Review

A Match and trace.

1.    ribbon

2.    pants

3.    pocket

4.    silver

B Look and circle.

1.    zipper
          silver

2.    ribbon
          button

Sentence Review

A Choose and write.

pockets	like	zippers

1.  They have big _____.

2. 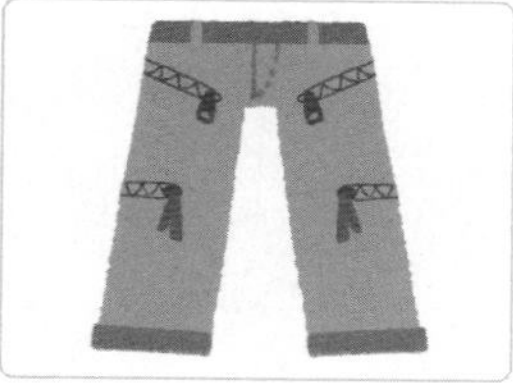 They have nice _____.

3.  I _____ these pants.

B Unscramble and write.

1. | a yellow | They | have | ribbon. |

➡ _____

2. | buttons. | silver | They | have |

➡ _____

3. | big! | They | too | are |

➡ _____

One Dark Night

Word Review

A Match and trace.

1.

on

2.

behind

3.

in

4.

under

B Look and circle.

1.
under
monster

2.
dark
in

Sentence Review

A Choose and write.

monsters	dark	on

1. There are scary _____ in my room.

2. Sometimes, it's _____ the chair.

3. It is a _____ night.

B Unscramble and write.

1. | Sometimes, | it's | the door. | behind |

   ➜ -

2. | under | the bed. | it's | Sometimes, |

   ➜ -

3. | your room. | are | no monsters | in | There |

   ➜ -

What I Want to Be

Word Review

A Match and trace.

1.

2.

3.

4.

want

many

doctor

baker

B Look and circle.

1.

police officer

baker

2.

doctor

baseball player

Sentence Review

A Choose and write.

many	want	doctor

1.  I want to be a _____ .

2.  I _____ to be a baseball player, too.

3.  I want to be _____ things!

B Unscramble and write.

1. | a police officer. | I | want | to be |

    → _____

2. | a baker, | want | to be | too. | I |

    → _____

3. | both? | Can | I | be |

    → _____

A Wonderful Museum

Word Review

A Match and trace.

1.

2.

3.

4.

castle

king

dinosaur

queen

B Look and circle.

1.
king

museum

2.
wonderful

castle

Sentence Review

A Choose and write.

| museum | castles | see |

1. We can see old _____ .

2. We can _____ dinosaurs.

3. Today, we go to a _____ .

B Unscramble and write.

1. | queens. | see | can | We |

   →

2. | can | We | see | cities. | old |

   →

3. | is | The museum | a wonderful | place. |

   →

Workbook | 워크북 정답

Unit 1. I Can Kick

■ Word Review

A **1.** see   **2.** hands

   3. legs   **4.** jump

B **1.** feet   **2.** kick

■ Sentences Review

A **1.** hands   **2.** have

   3. jump

B **1.** I can jump.

   2. I have two legs.

   3. I kicked too hard.

Unit 2. My Little Brother

■ Words Review

A **1.** baby   **2.** sit

   3. eat   **4.** sleep

B **1.** walk   **2.** brother

■ Sentences Review

A **1.** help   **2.** sleep

   3. eat

B **1.** I help him sit down.

   2. This is my baby brother.

   3. I love my little brother.

Unit 3. This Is My Family

■ Words Review

A **1.** father   **2.** sister

   3. student   **4.** dog

B **1.** family   **2.** mother

■ Sentences Review

A **1.** This   **2.** students

   3. dog

B **1.** This is my family.

   2. He is a cook.

   4. This is my sister, Jane.

Unit 4. School Is Fun

■ Words Review

A **1.** sing   **2.** write

   3. school   **4.** play

B **1.** draw   **2.** read

■ Sentences Review

A **1.** school   **2.** draw

   3. sing

B **1.** I read books.

   2. I write stories.

   3. I play with my friends.

26

Unit 5. Animals at Night

Words Review

A 1. hunt   2. bat
    3. owl   4. tiger

B 1. night   2. catch

Sentences Review

A 1. move   2. hunt
    3. Owls

B 1. Some animals move at night.
    2. They catch mice in the dark.
    3. Do you move at night, too?

Unit 6. The Four Seasons

Words Review

A 1. spring   2. warm
    3. fall   4. hot

B 1. summer   2. winter

Sentences Review

A 1. go   2. hot
    3. fishing

B 1. I go swimming.
    2. I go camping.
    3. It is spring.

Unit 7. What Flies in the Sky?

Words Review

A 1. kite   2. bee
    3. plane   4. sky

B 1. fly   2. balloon

Sentences Review

A 1. bee   2. sky
    3. fly

B 1. A balloon flies in the sky.
    2. What flies in the sky?
    3. A kite flies in the sky.

Unit 8. The Shape of Things

Words Review

A 1. square   2. triangle
    3. circle   4. rectangle

B 1. gift   2. clock

Sentences Review

A 1. triangle   2. rectangle
    3. clock

B 1. Shapes are everywhere.
    2. What is a square?
    3. The pizza is a circle.

Unit 9. Too Big

■ Words Review

Ⓐ **1.** ribbon   **2.** pocket

    3. pants   **4.** silver

Ⓑ **1.** zipper   **2.** button

■ Sentences Review

Ⓐ **1.** pockets   **2.** zippers

    3. like

Ⓑ **1.** They have a yellow ribbon.

    2. They have silver buttons.

    3. They are too big!

Unit 10. One Dark Night

■ Words Review

Ⓐ **1.** in   **2.** on

    3. behind   **4.** under

Ⓑ **1.** monster   **2.** dark

■ Sentences Review

Ⓐ **1.** monsters   **2.** on

    3. dark

Ⓑ **1.** Sometimes, it's behind the door.

    2. Sometimes, it's under the bed.

    3. There are no monsters in your room.

Unit 11. What I Want to Be

■ Words Review

Ⓐ **1.** doctor   **2.** baker

    3. want   **4.** many

Ⓑ **1.** police officer   **2.** baseball player

■ Sentences Review

Ⓐ **1.** doctor   **2.** want

    3. many

Ⓑ **1.** I want to be a police officer.

    2. I want to be a baker, too.

    3. Can I be both?

Unit 12. A Wonderful Museum

■ Words Review

Ⓐ **1.** queen   **2.** king

    3. castle   **4.** dinosaur

Ⓑ **1.** museum   **2.** wonderful

■ Sentences Review

Ⓐ **1.** castles   **2.** see

    3. museum

Ⓑ **1.** We can see queens.

    2. We can see old cities.

    3. The museum is a wonderful place.

READING

미국교과서 리딩

LEVEL 1 ①

Answer Key

길벗스쿨

Get Ready p.10

■ **Key Words** 단어를 듣고, 알맞은 사진을 가리키세요.

see 보다   hands 손   legs 다리

jump 점프하다   feet 발   kick 차다

■ **Quick Check** 단어를 완성하세요.

[h]ands   l[e][g]s

f[e][e]t   se[e]

■ **Key Sentence**

I have two hands. (나는 두 손이 있어요.)

듣고 따라 말한 후 알맞게 연결하세요.

I have two legs. (나는 두 다리가 있어요.) ⓒ

I have two eyes. (나는 두 눈이 있어요.) ⓐ

I have two feet. (나는 두 발이 있어요.) ⓑ

I have two ears. (나는 두 귀가 있어요.) ⓓ

■ **Quick Check** 알맞은 단어에 동그라미 하고 쓰세요.

I have two <u>feet</u>. (나는 두 발이 있어요.)

Now You Read p.12

나는 찰 수 있어요

나는 두 눈이 있어요.
나는 볼 수 있어요.

나는 두 손이 있어요.
나는 잡을 수 있어요.

나는 두 다리가 있어요.
나는 점프할 수 있어요.

나는 두 발이 있어요.
나는 찰 수 있어요.

오, 이런!
내가 너무 세게 찼어요.

■ **Pop Quiz**

남자아이는 지금 무엇을 하고 있나요?   축구(soccer)

Check Up p.14

■ **Comprehension** 다음을 읽고 알맞은 것에 체크하세요.

1. 이것은 _____ 에 대한 이야기예요.

☑ 나의 몸   □ 나의 공

2. 나는 두 _____이 있어요.

□ 입   ☑ 눈

3. 나는 발이 세 개 있어요.   False

4. 내가 너무 세게 찼어요.   True

■ **Sentence** 그림을 보고 문장에 알맞은 단어에 동그라미 하세요.

1. I can <u>kick</u>. (나는 찰 수 있어요.)

2. I can <u>jump</u>. (나는 점프할 수 있어요.)

3. I <u>kicked</u> too hard. (내가 너무 세게 찼어요.)

■ **Word** 퍼즐을 완성하세요.

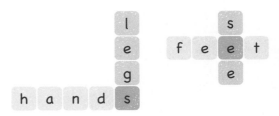

■ **Wrap-up** 관계 있는 것끼리 연결하고 알맞은 단어를 쓰세요.

1. ⓑ I have two hands. I can <u>catch</u>.
(나는 두 손이 있어요. 나는 잡을 수 있어요.)

2. ⓒ I have two legs. I can <u>jump</u>.
(나는 두 다리가 있어요. 나는 점프할 수 있어요.)

3. ⓐ I have two eyes. I can <u>see</u>.
(나는 두 눈이 있어요. 나는 볼 수 있어요.)

Get Ready p.16

■ **Key Words** 단어를 듣고, 알맞은 사진을 가리키세요.

baby 어린; 아기　　　brother 남자 형제(오빠, 형, 남동생)

eat 먹다　　　　　　walk 걷다

sit 앉다　　　　　　sleep 자다

■ **Quick Check** 단어를 완성하세요.

b[a]by　　　　s[l]eep

w[a]lk　　　　ea[t]

■ **Key Sentence**

I help him drink. (나는 그 애가 마시는 것을 도와줘요.)

듣고 따라 말한 후 알맞게 연결하세요.

I help him eat. (나는 그 애가 먹는 것을 도와줘요.) **c**

I help him walk. (나는 그 애가 걷는 것을 도와줘요.) **b**

I help him sit down. (나는 그 애가 앉는 것을 도와줘요.) **d**

I help him sleep. (나는 그 애가 자는 것을 도와줘요.) **a**

■ **Quick Check** 알맞은 단어에 동그라미 하고 쓰세요.

I help him walk. (나는 그 애가 걷는 것을 도와줘요.)

Now You Read p.18

나의 남동생

이 애는 나의 남동생이에요.
나는 그 애를 매일 도와줘요.

나는 그 애가 마시는 것을 도와줘요.
나는 그 애가 먹는 것을 도와줘요.

나는 그 애가 걷는 것을 도와줘요.
나는 그 애가 앉는 것을 도와줘요.
가끔 나는 그 애가 자는 것을 도와줘요.

나는 내 남동생을 사랑해요.

■ **Pop Quiz**

바닥에 무엇이 있나요?　　　곰 인형(a teddy bear)

Check Up p.20

■ **Comprehension** 다음을 읽고 알맞은 것에 체크하세요.

1. 이것은 _____에 대한 이야기예요.
　　□ 나의 여동생　　　☑ 나의 남동생

2. 나는 그 애를 _____ 도와줘요.
　　☑ 매일　　　　　　□ 일요일마다

3. 가끔 나는 그 애가 자는 것을 도와줘요.　　　True

4. 나는 그 애가 우는 것을 도와줘요.　　　False

■ **Sentence** 그림을 보고 문장에 알맞은 단어에 동그라미 하세요.

1. I help him <u>walk</u>. (나는 그 애가 걷는 것을 도와줘요.)

2. I help him <u>eat</u>. (나는 그 애가 먹는 것을 도와줘요.)

3. I <u>love</u> my little brother. (나는 내 남동생을 사랑해요.)

■ **Word** 단어를 찾아 동그라미 하세요.

w	n	h	p	b	a	b	y
a	e	s	o	a	q	e	i
l	e	s	l	e	e	p	k
k	a	e	n	f	a	h
a	t	o	n	g	c	m	g

■ **Wrap-up** 그림을 보고 알맞은 단어를 쓰세요.

1. I help him <u>drink</u>. (나는 그 애가 마시는 것을 도와줘요.)

2. I help him <u>eat</u>. (나는 그 애가 먹는 것을 도와줘요.)

3. I help him <u>walk</u>. (나는 그 애가 걷는 것을 도와줘요.)

4. I help him <u>sleep</u>. (나는 그 애가 자는 것을 도와줘요.)

Get Ready
p.22

■ **Key Words** 단어를 듣고, 알맞은 사진을 가리키세요.

family 가족   father 아빠

mother 엄마   sister 여자 형제(언니, 누나, 여동생)

student 학생   dog 개

■ **Quick Check** 단어를 완성하세요.

f amily   sis t er

fath e r   s t udent

■ **Key Sentence**

This is my family. (이것은 우리 가족이에요.)

듣고 따라 말한 후 알맞게 연결하세요.

This is my father. (이분은 우리 아빠예요.) **d**

This is my mother. (이분은 우리 엄마예요.) **a**

This is my sister. (이 아이는 내 여동생이에요.) **b**

This is my dog. (이것은 우리 개예요.) **c**

■ **Quick Check** 알맞은 단어에 동그라미 하고 쓰세요.

This is my sister. (이 아이는 내 여동생이에요.)

Now You Read
p.24

이것은 우리 가족이에요

이 사진을 보세요.
이것은 우리 가족이에요.

이분은 우리 아빠예요.
그는 요리사예요.

이분은 우리 엄마예요.
그녀는 선생님이에요.

이 아이는 내 여동생 제인이에요.
제인과 나는 이 학교의 학생이에요.

그리고 이것은 우리 개, 두기예요.

■ **Pop Quiz**

사진에서 제인에게 무엇이 있나요?

개 두기(a dog named Doogie)

Check Up
p.26

■ **Comprehension** 다음을 읽고 알맞은 것에 체크하세요.

1. 이것은 _____에 대한 이야기예요.
   □ 나의 학교   ☑ 나의 가족

2. 이것은 우리 _____, 두기예요.
   □ 고양이   ☑ 개

3. 우리 아빠는 선생님이에요.   False

4. 내 여동생은 학생이에요.   True

■ **Sentence** 그림을 보고 문장에 알맞은 단어에 동그라미 하세요.

1. This is my mother. (이분은 우리 엄마예요.)

2. This is my sister. (이 아이는 내 여동생이에요.)

3. Jane and I are students. (제인과 나는 학생이에요.)

■ **Word** 퍼즐을 완성하세요.

■ **Wrap-up** 그림을 보고 알맞은 단어를 쓰세요.

1. My father is a cook. (우리 아빠는 요리사예요.)

2. My mother is a teacher. (우리 엄마는 선생님이에요.)

3. My sister and I are students.
   (내 여동생과 나는 학생이에요.)

Get Ready
p.28

■ **Key Words** 단어를 듣고, 알맞은 사진을 가리키세요.

school 학교   read 읽다   write 쓰다

draw 그리다   sing 노래 부르다   play 놀다

■ **Quick Check** 단어를 완성하세요.

d r aw   wr i te

r ead   sin g

■ **Key Sentence**

I read books. (나는 책을 읽어요.)

듣고 따라 말한 후 알맞게 연결하세요.

I write stories. (나는 이야기를 써요.) ⓓ

I draw pictures. (나는 그림을 그려요.) ⓒ

I sing songs. (나는 노래를 불러요.) ⓑ

I eat my lunch. (나는 점심을 먹어요.) ⓐ

■ **Quick Check** 알맞은 단어에 동그라미 하고 쓰세요.

I draw pictures. (나는 그림을 그려요.)

Now You Read
p.30

학교는 재미있어요

여기는 우리 학교예요.

나는 학교에서 매우 재미있게 지내요.

나는 책을 읽어요.

나는 이야기를 써요.

나는 그림을 그려요.

나는 노래를 불러요.

나는 내 친구들과 놀아요.

나는 점심을 먹어요.

집에 갈 시간이에요.

내일 만나요!

Pop Quiz

여자아이는 무엇을 먹고 있나요?

샌드위치, 계란, 베이컨, 완두콩, 우유(a sandwich, an egg, bacons, peas, and milk)

Check Up
p.32

■ **Comprehension** 다음을 읽고 알맞은 것에 체크하세요.

1. 이것은 _____에 대한 이야기예요.

☐ 나의 집   ☑ 나의 학교

2. 나는 그림을 _____.

☐ 읽어요   ☑ 그려요

3. 나는 학교에서 매우 재미있게 지내요.   True

4. 나는 학교에서 내 남동생들과 놀아요.   False

■ **Sentence** 그림을 보고 문장에 알맞은 단어에 동그라미 하세요.

1. I write stories. (나는 이야기를 써요.)

2. I sing songs. (나는 노래를 불러요.)

3. This is my school. (여기는 우리 학교예요.)

■ **Word** 단어를 찾아 동그라미 하세요.

q	w	e	r	r	i	f	a
a	s	s	c	d	r	a	w
w	r	i	t	e	e	z	t
e	g	n	u	i	a	b	e
g	j	g	h	j	d	m	p

■ **Wrap-up** 그림을 보고 알맞은 단어를 쓰세요.

1. I write stories. (나는 이야기를 써요.)

2. I play with my friends. (나는 내 친구들과 놀아요.)

3. I eat my lunch. (나는 점심을 먹어요.)

4. I draw pictures. (나는 그림을 그려요.)

5. I read books. (나는 책을 읽어요.)

Get Ready
p.34

- **Key Words** 단어를 듣고, 알맞은 사진을 가리키세요.

night 밤	owl 올빼미, 부엉이	catch 잡다
bat 박쥐	tiger 호랑이	hunt 사냥하다

- **Quick Check** 단어를 완성하세요.

o wl

cat c h

ti g er

nig h t

- **Key Sentence**

Some animals move at night. (어떤 동물은 밤에 활동해요.)

듣고 따라 말한 후 알맞게 연결하세요.

Owls move at night. (올빼미는 밤에 활동해요.) ⓒ

Bats move at night. (박쥐는 밤에 활동해요.) ⓐ

Tigers move at night. (호랑이는 밤에 활동해요.) ⓑ

Cats move at night. (고양이는 밤에 활동해요.) ⓓ

- **Quick Check** 알맞은 단어에 동그라미 하고 쓰세요.

Bats move at night. (박쥐는 밤에 활동해요.)

Now You Read
p.36

밤의 동물

어떤 동물은 밤에 활동해요.

올빼미는 밤에 활동해요.
그들은 어둠 속에서 쥐를 잡아요.

박쥐는 밤에 활동해요.
그들은 어둠 속에서 과일을 먹어요.

호랑이는 밤에 활동해요.
그들은 어둠 속에서 사슴을 사냥해요.

당신도 밤에 활동하나요?

- **Pop Quiz**

올빼미는 무엇을 잡고 있나요?   쥐(a mouse)

Check Up
p.38

- **Comprehension** 다음을 읽고 알맞은 것에 체크하세요.

1. 이것은 _____에 대한 이야기예요.
   ☑ 밤의 동물   ☐ 동물원의 동물

2. _____는 밤에 활동해요.
   ☐ 나비   ☑ 호랑이

3. 박쥐는 밤에 활동해요.   True

4. 올빼미는 어둠 속에서 사슴을 사냥해요.   False

- **Sentence** 그림을 보고 문장에 알맞은 단어에 동그라미 하세요.

1. Some animals move at <u>night</u>. (어떤 동물은 밤에 활동해요.)

2. They eat <u>fruits</u> in the dark.
   (그들은 어둠 속에서 과일을 먹어요.)

3. They catch <u>mice</u> in the dark.
   (그들은 어둠 속에서 쥐를 잡아요.)

- **Word** 퍼즐을 완성하세요.

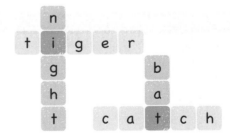

- **Wrap-up** 관계 있는 것끼리 연결하고 알맞은 단어를 쓰세요.

1. ⓒ <u>Owls</u> catch mice in the dark.
   (올빼미는 어둠 속에서 쥐를 잡아요.)

2. ⓑ <u>Tigers</u> hunt deer in the dark.
   (호랑이는 어둠 속에서 사슴을 사냥해요.)

3. ⓐ <u>Bats</u> eat fruits in the dark.
   (박쥐는 어둠 속에서 과일을 먹어요.)

Get Ready
p.40

- **Key Words** 단어를 듣고, 알맞은 사진을 가리키세요.

spring 봄   warm 따뜻한   summer 여름
hot 더운   fall 가을   winter 겨울

- **Quick Check** 단어를 완성하세요.

[s]pring   su[m]mer
fa[l]l   win[t]er

- **Key Sentence**

I go fishing. (나는 낚시를 하러 가요.)

듣고 따라 말한 후 알맞게 연결하세요.
I go swimming. (나는 수영을 하러 가요.) **c**
I go camping. (나는 캠핑을 하러 가요.) **b**
I go skating. (나는 스케이트를 타러 가요.) **d**
I go skiing. (나는 스키를 타러 가요.) **a**

- **Quick Check** 알맞은 단어에 동그라미 하고 쓰세요.

I go swimming. (나는 수영을 하러 가요.)

Now You Read
p.42

사계절

봄이에요.
날씨가 따뜻해요.
나는 낚시를 하러 가요.

여름이에요.
날씨가 더워요.
나는 수영을 하러 가요.

가을이에요.
날씨가 시원해요.
나는 캠핑을 하러 가요.

겨울이에요.
날씨가 추워요.
나는 스케이트를 타러 가요.

- **Pop Quiz**

아이들 몇 명이 낚시를 하고 있나요?   세 명(three kids)

Check Up
p.44

- **Comprehension** 다음을 읽고 알맞은 것에 체크하세요.

1. 이것은 _____에 대한 이야기예요.
   □ 친구 네 명   ☑ 사계절

2. 봄이에요. 나는 _____ 가요.
   ☑ 낚시를 하러   □ 스케이트를 타러

3. 여름이에요. 날씨가 추워요.   False

4. 가을이에요. 날씨가 시원해요.   True

- **Sentence** 그림을 보고 문장에 알맞은 단어에 동그라미 하세요.

1. I go skating. (나는 스케이트를 타러 가요.)
2. I go camping. (나는 캠핑을 하러 가요.)
3. The weather is hot. (날씨가 더워요.)

- **Word** 단어를 찾아 동그라미 하세요.

f	w	h	w	c	j	s	c
a	s	p	r	i	n	g	w
l	b	m	t	d	f	w	a
l	v	n	a	b	k	s	r
a	w	i	n	t	e	r	m

- **Wrap-up** 그림을 보고 알맞은 단어를 쓰세요.

1. I go swimming. (나는 수영을 하러 가요.)
2. I go fishing. (나는 낚시를 하러 가요.)
3. I go skating. (나는 스케이트를 타러 가요.)
4. I go camping. (나는 캠핑을 하러 가요.)

Get Ready   p.46

- **Key Words** 단어를 듣고, 알맞은 사진을 가리키세요.

  | fly 날다 | sky 하늘 | balloon 풍선 |
  | bee 벌 | kite 연 | plane 비행기 |

- **Quick Check** 단어를 완성하세요.

  ball o o n   p lane
  k i te   f ly

- **Key Sentence**

  A plane flies in the sky. (비행기가 하늘을 날아요.)

  듣고 따라 말한 후 알맞게 연결하세요.
  A balloon flies in the sky. (풍선이 하늘을 날아요.) **d**
  A bee flies in the sky. (벌이 하늘을 날아요.) **c**
  A kite flies in the sky. (연이 하늘을 날아요.) **a**
  A bird flies in the sky. (새가 하늘을 날아요.) **b**

- **Quick Check** 알맞은 단어에 동그라미 하고 쓰세요.

  A kite flies in the sky. (연이 하늘을 날아요.)

Now You Read   p.48

하늘을 나는 것은 무엇인가요?

저것이 보이나요?
하늘을 나는 것은 무엇인가요?

풍선이 하늘을 날아요.
벌이 하늘을 날아요.

연이 하늘을 날아요.
비행기가 하늘을 날아요.

나도 하늘을 날 수 있다면 좋겠어요!

- **Pop Quiz**

  풍선 색깔은 무엇인가요?   빨간색(red)

Check Up   p.50

- **Comprehension** 다음을 읽고 알맞은 것에 체크하세요.

1. 이것은 무엇이 _____을 나는지에 대한 이야기예요.
   □ 물   ☑ 하늘

2. _____이(가) 하늘을 날아요.
   ☑ 풍선   □ 호랑이

3. 벌이 하늘을 날아요.   True

4. 나도 하늘에서 수영할 수 있다면 좋겠어요!   False

- **Sentence** 그림을 보고 문장에 알맞은 단어에 동그라미 하세요.

1. A kite flies in the sky. (연이 하늘을 날아요.)
2. A plane flies in the sky. (비행기가 하늘을 날아요.)
3. I wish I could fly in the sky!
   (나도 하늘을 날 수 있다면 좋겠어요!)

- **Word** 퍼즐을 완성하세요.

- **Wrap-up** 단어를 읽고 빈칸에 해당하는 것에 동그라미 하세요.

  A _____ flies in the sky. (~이(가) 하늘을 날아요.)

  bee (벌)
  kite (연)
  plane (비행기)
  bat (박쥐)
  balloon (풍선)

The Shape of Things 사물의 모양

Get Ready p.52

■ **Key Words** 단어를 듣고, 알맞은 사진을 가리키세요.

circle 동그라미, 원형   square 정사각형

clock 시계   rectangle 직사각형

gift 선물   triangle 세모, 삼각형

■ **Quick Check** 단어를 완성하세요.

t r iangle   c l ock

g ift   c ircle

■ **Key Sentence**

The pizza is a circle. (피자는 동그라미예요.)

듣고 따라 말한 후 알맞게 연결하세요.

The clock is a square. (시계는 정사각형이에요.) **c**

The plate is a circle. (접시는 동그라미예요.) **d**

The party hat is a triangle. (파티 모자는 세모예요.) **b**

The gift box is a rectangle. (선물 상자는 직사각형이에요.) **a**

■ **Quick Check** 알맞은 단어에 동그라미 하고 쓰세요.

The gift box is a rectangle. (선물 상자는 직사각형이에요.)

Now You Read p.54

사물의 모양

모양은 어디에나 있어요.
그것들을 찾아봐요.

무엇이 동그라미인가요?
피자가 동그라미예요.

무엇이 정사각형인가요?
시계가 정사각형이에요.

무엇이 직사각형인가요?
선물 상자가 직사각형이에요.

무엇이 세모인가요?
파티 모자가 세모예요.

■ **Pop Quiz**

지금은 몇 시인가요?   9시 30분(nine thirty)

Check Up p.56

■ **Comprehension** 다음을 읽고 알맞은 것에 체크하세요.

1. 이것은 사물들의 _____에 대한 이야기예요.
   ☑ 모양   □ 색깔

2. 피자는 _____이에요(예요).
   □ 정사각형   ☑ 동그라미

3. 모양은 어디에나 있어요.   True

4. 선물 상자는 세모예요.   False

■ **Sentence** 그림을 보고 문장에 알맞은 단어에 동그라미 하세요.

1. Shapes are everywhere. (모양은 어디에나 있어요.)

2. The party hat is a triangle. (파티 모자는 세모예요.)

3. The clock is a square. (시계는 정사각형이에요.)

■ **Word** 단어를 찾아 동그라미 하세요.

c	i	r	c	l	e	t	o
l	g	w	h	j	m	f	f
o	i	s	q	u	a	r	e
c	f	x	o	q	r	d	f
k	t	b	c	d	y	h	p

■ **Wrap-up** 관계 있는 것끼리 연결하고 알맞은 단어를 쓰세요.

1. **d** The party hat is a triangle. (파티 모자는 세모예요.)

2. **c** The gift box is a rectangle.
   (선물 상자는 직사각형이에요.)

3. **a** The pizza is a circle. (피자는 동그라미예요.)

4. **b** The clock is a square. (시계는 정사각형이에요.)

Get Ready
p.58

- **Key Words** 단어를 듣고, 알맞은 사진을 가리키세요.

pants 바지　　　silver 은색의; 은　　　button 단추

ribbon 리본　　　pocket 주머니　　　zipper 지퍼

- **Quick Check** 단어를 완성하세요.

| b utton | pocke t |
| p ants | z ipper |

- **Key Sentence**

They have silver buttons. (그것은 은색 단추가 있어요.)

듣고 따라 말한 후 알맞게 연결하세요.

They have big pockets. (그것은 큰 주머니가 있어요.) **a**

They have nice zippers. (그것은 멋진 지퍼가 있어요.) **c**

It has a yellow ribbon. (그것은 노란 리본이 있어요.) **b**

It has red lace. (그것은 빨간 레이스가 있어요.) **d**

- **Quick Check** 알맞은 단어에 동그라미 하고 쓰세요.

It has big pockets. (그것은 큰 주머니가 있어요.)

Now You Read
p.60

너무 커요

나는 이 바지가 마음에 들어요.

그것은 나한테 잘 어울릴 거예요.

그것은 은색 단추가 있어요.

그것은 노란 리본이 있어요.

그것은 큰 주머니가 있어요.

그것은 멋진 지퍼가 있어요.

그것은 나에게 완벽하게 어울릴 거예요.

오, 이런!

그것은 너무 커요!

- **Pop Quiz**

바지에 은색 단추가 몇 개 있나요?　　두 개(two buttons)

Check Up
p.62

- **Comprehension** 다음을 읽고 알맞은 것에 체크하세요.

1. 이것은 _____에 대한 이야기예요.
   ☑ 내 바지　　　□ 내 셔츠

2. 나는 이 바지가(를) _____.
   ☑ 마음에 들어요　　　□ 그려요

3. 그것은 은색 단추들이 있어요.　　　True

4. 그것은 너무 작아요!　　　False

- **Sentence** 그림을 보고 문장에 알맞은 단어에 동그라미 하세요.

1. It has a yellow ribbon. (그것은 노란 리본이 있어요.)

2. They have big pockets. (그것은 큰 주머니가 있어요.)

3. They have nice zippers. (그것은 멋진 지퍼가 있어요.)

- **Word** 퍼즐을 완성하세요.

- **Wrap-up** 그림을 보고 알맞은 단어를 쓰세요.

I like these pants. (나는 이 바지가 마음에 들어요.)

1. They have big pockets. (그것은 큰 주머니가 있어요.)

2. They have silver buttons. (그것은 은색 단추가 있어요.)

3. They have a yellow ribbon. (그것은 노란 리본이 있어요.)

4. They have nice zippers. (그것은 멋진 지퍼가 있어요.)

Get Ready
p.64

■ **Key Words** 단어를 듣고, 알맞은 사진을 가리키세요.

dark 깜깜한	monster 괴물	in ~안에
under ~아래에	on ~위에	behind ~뒤에

■ **Quick Check** 단어를 완성하세요.

m onster   d ark

un d er   behin d

■ **Key Sentence**

It's under the bed. (그것은 침대 아래에 있어요.)

듣고 따라 말한 후 알맞게 연결하세요.

It's on the chair. (그것은 의자 위에 있어요.) **d**

It's in the closet. (그것은 옷장 안에 있어요.) **b**

It's behind the door. (그것은 문 뒤에 있어요.) **c**

It's on the desk. (그것은 책상 위에 있어요.) **a**

■ **Quick Check** 알맞은 단어에 동그라미 하고 쓰세요.

It's in the closet. (그것은 옷장 안에 있어요.)

Now You Read
p.66

어느 깜깜한 밤

깜깜한 밤이에요.
내 방에 무서운 괴물이 있어요.

때로는 그것이 침대 아래에 있어요.
때로는 그것이 의자 위에 있어요.

때로는 그것이 옷장 안에 있어요.
때로는 그것이 문 뒤에 있어요.

얘야, 무서워하지 말거라.
네 방에 괴물은 하나도 없단다.

■ **Pop Quiz**

괴물이 몇 마리 보이나요?   네 마리(four monsters)

Check Up
p.68

■ **Comprehension** 다음을 읽고 알맞은 것에 체크하세요.

1. 이것은 _____ 에 대한 이야기예요.
   - ☑ 깜깜한 밤
   - ☐ 비 오는 날

2. 내 방에 무서운 _____이 있어요.
   - ☐ 박쥐들
   - ☑ 괴물들

3. 괴물이 침대 위에 있어요.   False

4. 괴물이 옷장 안에 있어요.   True

■ **Sentence** 그림을 보고 문장에 알맞은 단어에 동그라미 하세요.

1. It's on the chair. (그것은 의자 위에 있어요.)
2. It's behind the door. (그것은 문 뒤에 있어요.)
3. It is a dark night. (깜깜한 밤이에요.)

■ **Word** 단어를 찾아 동그라미 하세요.

u	p	b	e	h	i	n	d
n	s	p	e	x	a	d	a
d	h	o	u	c	g	l	r
e	f	r	d	v	s	j	k
r	m	o	n	s	t	e	r

■ **Wrap-up** 그림을 보고 알맞은 단어를 쓰세요.

Sometimes, it's _____.
(때로는, 그것이 ~에 있어요.)

1. behind the door (문 뒤)
2. under the bed (침대 아래)
3. on the chair (의자 위)
4. in the closet (옷장 안)

What I Want to Be 내가 되고 싶은 것

Get Ready

■ Key Words 단어를 듣고, 알맞은 사진을 가리키세요.

want 원하다   doctor 의사

baseball player 야구 선수   police officer 경찰관

baker 제빵사   many 많은

■ Quick Check 단어를 완성하세요.

d o ctor   b a ker

w ant   p olice off i cer

■ Key Sentence

I want to be a doctor. (나는 의사가 되고 싶어요.)

듣고 따라 말한 후 알맞게 연결하세요.

I want to be a baseball player.
(나는 야구 선수가 되고 싶어요.) ⓒ

I want to be a police officer. (나는 경찰관이 되고 싶어요.) ⓑ

I want to be a baker. (나는 제빵사가 되고 싶어요.) ⓓ

I want to be a singer. (나는 가수가 되고 싶어요.) ⓐ

■ Quick Check 알맞은 단어에 동그라미 하고 쓰세요.

I want to be a baker. (나는 제빵사가 되고 싶어요.)

Now You Read

내가 되고 싶은 것

나는 의사가 되고 싶어요.
나는 야구 선수도 되고 싶어요.
둘 다 될 수 있을까요?

나는 경찰관이 되고 싶어요.
나는 제빵사도 되고 싶어요.
둘 다 될 수 있을까요?

오, 나는 되고 싶은 것이 많아요!

■ Pop Quiz

가스 오븐 위에 무엇이 있나요?   빨간색 냄비(a red pan)

Check Up

■ Comprehension 다음을 읽고 알맞은 것에 체크하세요.

1. 이것은 내가 되고 _____ 것에 대한 이야기예요.
   ☑ 싶은   ☐ 싶지 않은

2. 나는 _____이(가) 되고 싶어요.
   ☑ 경찰관   ☐ 간호사

3. 나는 선생님이 되고 싶어요.   False

4. 나는 되고 싶은 것이 많아요.   True

■ Sentence 그림을 보고 문장에 알맞은 단어에 동그라미 하세요.

1. I want to be a baseball player.
   (나는 야구 선수가 되고 싶어요.)

2. I want to be a police officer. (나는 경찰관이 되고 싶어요.)

3. I want to be many things. (나는 되고 싶은 것이 많아요.)

■ Word 퍼즐을 완성하세요.

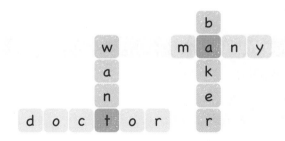

■ Wrap-up 단어를 읽고 빈칸에 해당하는 것에 동그라미 하세요.

I want to be a _____. (나는 ~이(가) 되고 싶어요.)

baker (제빵사)

baseball player (야구 선수)

doctor (의사)

police officer (경찰관)

A Wonderful Museum
아주 멋진 박물관

Get Ready p.76

■ **Key Words** 단어를 듣고, 알맞은 사진을 가리키세요.

museum 박물관   castle 성   king 왕

queen 여왕   dinosaur 공룡   wonderful 아주 멋진

■ **Quick Check** 단어를 완성하세요.

[c]astle   ki[n][g]

[d]inosaur   qu[e][e]n

■ **Key Sentence**

We can see old cities. (우리는 오래된 도시를 볼 수 있어요.)

듣고 따라 말한 후 알맞게 연결하세요.

We can see old castles. (우리는 오래된 성을 볼 수 있어요.) ⓑ

We can see kings. (우리는 왕을 볼 수 있어요.) ⓐ

We can see dinosaurs. (우리는 공룡을 볼 수 있어요.) ⓒ

We can see mummies. (우리는 미라를 볼 수 있어요.) ⓓ

■ **Quick Check** 알맞은 단어에 동그라미 하고 쓰세요.

We can see old castles. (우리는 오래된 성을 볼 수 있어요.)

Now You Read p.78

아주 멋진 박물관

오늘 우리는 박물관에 가요.
우리는 무엇을 볼 수 있을까요?

우리는 오래된 도시를 볼 수 있어요.
우리는 오래된 성을 볼 수 있어요.

우리는 왕을 볼 수 있어요.
우리는 여왕을 볼 수 있어요.

우리는 공룡을 볼 수 있어요.
그리고 우리는 미라를 볼 수 있어요.

박물관은 아주 멋진 곳이에요.

■ **Pop Quiz**

왕은 머리에 무엇을 쓰고 있나요?   왕관(a crown)

Check Up p.80

■ **Comprehension** 다음을 읽고 알맞은 것에 체크하세요.

1. 이것은 _____에 대한 이야기예요.
   □ 공룡   ☑ 박물관

2. 우리는 오래된 _____를 볼 수 있어요.
   ☑ 도시   □ 자동차

3. 오늘 우리는 박물관에 가요.   True

4. 우리는 박물관에서 호랑이들을 볼 수 있어요.   False

■ **Sentence** 그림을 보고 문장에 알맞은 단어에 동그라미 하세요.

1. We can see kings. (우리는 왕을 볼 수 있어요.)

2. We can see mummies. (우리는 미라를 볼 수 있어요.)

3. The museum is a wonderful place.
   (박물관은 아주 멋진 곳이에요.)

■ **Word** 단어를 찾아 동그라미 하세요.

q	c	a	s	t	l	e	k
u	n	d	e	m	n	o	i
e	x	f	j	a	o	a	n
e	r	b	d	b	t	f	g
n	y	m	u	s	e	u	m

■ **Wrap-up** 그림을 보고 관계 있는 것끼리 연결하세요.

1. We can see kings. (우리는 왕을 볼 수 있어요.) ⓑ

2. We can see dinosaurs. (우리는 공룡을 볼 수 있어요.) ⓐ

3. We can see mummies. (우리는 미라를 볼 수 있어요.) ⓓ

4. We can see old castles.
   (우리는 오래된 성을 볼 수 있어요.) ⓒ

미국교과서 READING Level 1 권별 리딩 주제

1권 1.1

1. Body Parts
2. My Brother
3. Family
4. My School
5. Animals
6. Seasons
7. Things in the Sky
8. Shapes
9. Clothes
10. Monsters
11. Jobs
12. Museum

2권 1.2

1. Rain
2. Spring
3. Things in Pairs
4. Animal Homes
5. Community
6. My Room
7. Bad Dream
8. Colors
9. Food
10. Transportation
11. Friends
12. Sense of Touch

3권 1.3

1. Tree
2. Housework
3. Riding a Bike
4. Spider
5. Hobbies
6. Winter
7. Vegetables
8. Sea
9. My Town
10. School Tools
11. Farm Animals
12. Five Senses

길벗스쿨 공식 카페, <기적의 공부방>에서 함께 공부해요!

기적의 학습단

홈스쿨링 응원 프로젝트! 학습단에 참여하여 공부 습관도 기르고 칭찬 선물도 받으세요!

도서 서평단

길벗스쿨의 책을 가장 먼저 체험하고, 기획에도 직접 참여해 보세요.

알찬 학습 팁

엄마표 학습 노하우를 나누며 우리 아이 맞춤 학습법을 함께 찾아요.

<기적의 공부방> https://cafe.naver.com/gilbutschool